It's a Wonderful Life Study Guide

A Bible Study Based on the
Christmas Classic
It's a Wonderful Life

By Alan Vermilye

It's a Wonderful Life Study Guide:
A Bible Study Based on the Christmas Classic *It's a Wonderful Life*

Copyright © 2019 Alan Vermilye
Brown Chair Books

ISBN-13: 978-1-948481-10-6

To learn more about this Bible study, to order additional copies, or to download the answer guide, visit **www.BrownChairBooks.com**.

Version 1

Table of Contents

Introduction

Each year growing up, Christmas dinner was served promptly at noon at my grandmother's home. It was a small house that somehow accommodated a large family and more food than we could possibly eat. All the adults would squeeze around the makeshift dining table that was assembled in the living room, and the kids would settle in an even smaller den to begin our holiday feast. Fortunately, being one of the older kids, I received seating rights in my grandmother's recliner, positioned directly in front of the television. It was the one day all year that I was allowed to sit in front of the television and eat. It was great!

This was also during a time when there was no cable television or unlimited video streaming options available, just five or six channels to choose from. So somehow we always seemed to settle on *It's a Wonderful Life*.

Year after year, I was captivated by the story of George Bailey of Bedford Falls, whose life does not turn out quite as he expects. He's a dreamer, likable, and incredibly selfless but also suffers scandal and ruin not of his own making, which leads him to contemplate suicide. But through the supernatural intervention of God and the love of family and friends, his life is saved at the end. And by the way, this miraculous final act just happens to occur on Christmas Eve, as all good miracles should!

Even as a young adult, I still felt compelled to watch the show each Christmas, and I desired for those around me to enjoy this cinematic classic as much as I did. In fact, as newlyweds, I positioned my very understanding wife in a folding chair to watch it with me because she kept falling asleep on prior attempts! Now, over twenty-five years later, it's part of our family's Christmas tradition to watch the movie each year with our kids.

For many, the film is no more than "Capra Corn," a term used to describe the sentimental and feel-good themes found in many of Frank Capra's films. Others simply watch it out of Christmas tradition while sipping eggnog in front of a roaring fire.

For me, it's always been about much more. It's a stark reminder that every life is important no matter how big or how small. On the surface, George Bailey appears to be nothing more than an average middle-aged man living a normal life in a small-town community. But in fact, his life had significant value and impact on his family, his community, and, yes, even the world.

It's a battle between good and evil, selflessness and selfishness, and a story of faith, family, and friends. It's the story of loving others so much that you would give up your self-interest for theirs even when it costs you everything—maybe even your life.

This, of course, makes it the perfect Christmas movie and a wonderful demonstration of selfless love. George Bailey loved his neighbor as himself—probably even more so. He was not perfect, and he made mistakes, even one that almost cost him his life. However, in the end, he found that his sacrifice for others resulted in their sacrifice for him. He truly had a wonderful life, a life that no amount of money can buy.

I can think of no better movie to watch at Christmas.

Course Notes and Study Format

It's a Wonderful Life Bible Study Guide is divided up into five weekly study sessions with discussion questions structured to be highly flexible for group or individual study.

How to Use This Study Guide

The study is ideal for Sunday school classes as well as midweek times at the church or in the homes of group members. Session length is variable, but ideally, you should allow at least 60 minutes per session. If you feel that you cannot get through all the questions in a single session, pick and choose the questions you want to make sure you cover.

It's most helpful for learning purposes if each person has their own book and works through the study questions prior to each class. However, couples might find it convenient to share a book.

Since the Bible study is based on the movie, it's recommended to watch the film either individually or as a group prior to beginning the study. Even those who have seen the movie multiple times will benefit from a fresh viewing.

Free Downloadable Video

Each weekly session has several free video segments that correspond with discussion questions. These segments have been compiled into one video session for each week. You can download these videos for free at the link below. You will also find Vimeo links that allow you to stream each session.

Video download link: www.BrownChairBooks.com/videos

Each weekly segment is between 7–10 minutes of total video run time and there are markers on each video session so that you can pause between each segment. Videos segments in each session are identified by the icon below.

If you are not able to use the videos in your setting, segments of the movie script are printed in each session to guide you through the discussion questions.

Answers and Scripture References

The answers to each question as well as a Scripture Reference Guide can be found at www.BrownChairBooks.com. However, do not cheat yourself. Work through each session prior to viewing the answers. The Scripture Reference Guide is a handy tool that saves time in class spent looking up Bible passages.

Book Summary

Set in Upstate New York during the first half of the 20th century, *It's a Wonderful Life* takes place in the fictional town of Bedford Falls during the dramatic economic downturn of the Great Depression followed by the United States' entry into World War II.

The movie opens one Christmas Eve on the snowy and deserted streets of Bedford Falls as the community is petitioning the heavens to help the story's protagonist and beloved town hero, George Bailey. George, overcome with despair, drunkenly staggers to a bridge on which he contemplates his own self-destruction. The story unfolds with a retrospective look at the critical moments in George's life taken for the benefit of his guardian angel, Clarence Odbody, who, if he successfully saves George, will earn his wings.

From the time he was a young boy, George was a dreamer who wanted to travel to exotic places, have adventures, go to college, and build monumental skyscrapers and bridges. However, his responsibilities to his family and community of Bedford Falls keep him from fulfilling those dreams.

Reluctantly, he becomes a respectable citizen following in the footsteps of his father, running the family business, the Bailey Building and Loan. This business serves the working class of Bedford Falls as their only hope of buying their own homes.

The bank and many of the other local businesses are run or controlled by George's nemesis, Mr. Potter, a greedy, merciless businessman. Mr. Potter is not interested in lending money to poor people, since he prefers that they be stuck renting the horrible shacks that he also owns.

George has a wonderful family, including his kind and loving wife, Mary, and their four healthy children. He is well loved in the community, treats everyone with dignity and respect, and helps out whenever he can.

Then, on Christmas Eve, through no fault of his own, George's business comes up short in their accounts by a substantial amount of money. Unbeknownst to George, this money was accidently misplaced into the hands of Mr. Potter by George's forgetful business partner, Uncle Billy. As a result, George finds himself confronted with a financial crisis that threatens to ruin his business, his home, his standing with the community, and, ultimately, his life.

Cornered by Mr. Potter, a bank examiner, and the authorities, George is now facing arrest for bank fraud and misappropriation of funds. Having exhausted all of his resources in efforts to recover or replace the money, George believes his best avenue for escape is to end his life in the cold and dark rivers of Bedford Falls.

In his moment of crisis, Clarence intervenes to convince the incredulous George of the value of "God's greatest gift." In order to prove to George that his life is important, Clarence decides to grant him his self-pitying wish and show him what Bedford Falls would have been like if he had never been born.

Clarence unveils a nightmare scene of the moral degradation of Bedford Falls in George's absence. Without George, his brother, Harry, dies at the age of nine in a sledding accident since George was not there to save him, the Building and Loan goes out of business after his father's death, the houses in Bailey Park are never built for the working class of Bedford Falls, Mr. Gower is sent to prison for accidentally poisoning a child and later becomes a beggar, Mary never gets married and becomes an old maid, George's kids do not exist, Uncle Billy goes insane, George's mother has to open a boarding house to survive, Violet becomes a scandalous prostitute, Ernie the cab driver's wife leaves him, and the town of Bedford Falls is totally dominated by Mr. Potter and becomes a place of gin mills, pool halls, and gentlemen's clubs called Pottersville.

George would also learn that his impact stretched far beyond this small town. George's brother, Harry, won the Congressional Medal of Honor for shooting down enemy fire and saving the lives of every man on a transport during the war. Without George to save Harry as a child, every man on the transport died.

Because of Clarence's influence, George understands that the dark alternate reality of Pottersville is not the result of something going fundamentally wrong with the world; it's simply the way things would be had he not been there to prevent them.

Finally, unable to face what might have been, George begs to live again and return to his life even though it means bankruptcy, financial ruin, and prison. Once again, George is granted his wish and rushes home. He ecstatically greets his kids and Mary followed by an entourage of friends and family all coming to his rescue. Through the generous donations of his friends and fellow townsman, all of the lost money is recouped. As a bell on the Christmas tree rings, his daughter Zuzu says that every time a bell rings an angel receives his wings, and George knows that this time it is Clarence.

Through this experience, Clarence is able to slowly convince George that his life is still worth living and that the most valuable things in life have little to do with money. In fact, George discovers that even in the worst of times, he is the richest man in town when it comes to the things that really matter.

Character Summary

GEORGE BAILEY – Played by Jimmy Stewart

George is the honest, good-hearted, and compassionate hero of Bedford Falls who dreams of traveling the world, having adventures, and building monumental skyscrapers and bridges. He spends his whole life trying to get out of Bedford Falls, but each time he seems to have a chance, he ends up having to stay because of things that happen beyond his control. One Christmas, as George's life seems to be falling apart, he is visited by Clarence, an angel who helps him to see how much his life has truly been worth by granting his wish of having never been born. Through a series of nightmarish scenes unveiled by Clarence, George finally learns that all he's ever needed or wanted he already has when surrounded by his loving family and friends.

MARY HATCH BAILEY – Played by Donna Reed

Mary is the kind, sweet, innocent wife of George who eventually becomes the mother of their four children. She has loved George since they were children and proves her love by becoming a faithful, loving, and devoted wife. Even in George's darkest hour, she is his strength and helps him see that the most important things in life are not found outside of Bedford Falls.

MR. HENRY F. POTTER – Played by Lionel Barrymore

Mr. Potter is a mean, greedy, and merciless businessman and powerful banker who owns most of Bedford Falls. He has no family and has spent his whole life accumulating money and power. He is George's nemesis. He sees the Building and Loan as competition to his own businesses and wants it eliminated.

CLARENCE ODBODY AS2 – Played by Henry Travers
Clarence is George's energetic guardian angel. He is an angel second class (AS2) because he has not yet helped enough people to "earn his wings." When George faces his greatest life crisis, Clarence is sent by God to open George's eyes and save his life. He does so by granting George's request to have never been born. In the end, George chooses life, and Clarence gets his wings.

WILLIAM "UNCLE BILLY" BAILEY – Played by Thomas Mitchell
Uncle Billy is George's sweet but absent-minded uncle and business partner at the Bailey Building and Loan. He is a kind but nervous man who was not competent enough to keep the business afloat after his brother Peter's death, leading George to abandon his dreams to run the family business instead. Later, Uncle Billy's hapless action of losing a considerable amount of money belonging to the Building and Loan leads George down a destructive path.

PETER BAILEY – Played by Samuel S. Hinds
Peter Bailey is the father of George and Harry. Although he was a good father and a decent man, he was not a very good businessman. He started the Bailey Building and Loan with his brother Billy to loan money to working people so they could buy houses. His sudden death interrupts George's dreams of escape the small town of Bedford Falls.

HARRY BAILEY – Played by Todd Karns
Harry is George's younger brother who goes off to college while George stays in town to help run the Building and Loan. George saved his life in a sledding accident when they were kids.

MRS. BAILEY – Played by Beulah Bondi
Mrs. Bailey is George's sweet and loving mother who relies on George for financial support after the death of her husband.

MR. GOWER – Played by H.B. Warner
Mr. Gower is the owner of the town drugstore where George worked as a kid. In a moment of deep depression from the loss of his son, Mr. Gower nearly poisons a child only to be stopped by a young George Bailey.

VIOLET BICK – Played by Gloria Grahame
Violet is a sexy young woman who catches the eyes of most men when she walks by. She has been fond of George since they were kids.

SAM WAINWRIGHT – Played by Frank Albertson
Sam is a childhood friend of George and Harry who later becomes a successful businessman.

ERNIE THE TAXI DRIVER – Played by Frank Faylen
Ernie is George's friend and the town's cab driver.

BERT THE COP – Played by Ward Bond
Bert is George's friend and the local town cop.

ANNIE – Played by Lillian Randolph
Annie is the Bailey family's maid.

NICK THE BARTENDER – Played by Sheldon Leonard
Nick is George's friend and the bartender at Martini's Bar.

MR. MARTINI – Played by William Edmunds
Mr. Martini is the Italian immigrant who owns the town bar and whom George helps his family get a house in Bailey Park.

GEORGE'S KIDS
Zuzu played by Karolyn Grimes
Ruth played by Virginia Patton
Peter played by Larry Simms
Tommy played by Jimmy Hawkins

Session 1: I'm Gonna See the World!

Consider a scenario where you've planned the ultimate family vacation. You've worked hard all year saving money. You've read books, researched online, and created the perfect travel itinerary. With confidence, you book your non-refundable flights, reserve the ideal hotel, and get the family packed and ready to go. Just as you're ready to leave on this dream vacation, an expected situation derails the entire trip, and you lose all the money and time you invested.

The Best Laid Plans...

I know what I'm gonna do tomorrow, and the next day, and the next year, and the year after that. I'm shakin' the dust of this crummy little town off my feet and I'm gonna see the world. Italy, Greece, the Parthenon, the Colosseum. Then, I'm comin' back here *to go to college and see what they know. And then I'm gonna build things. I'm gonna build airfields, I'm gonna build skyscrapers a hundred stories high, I'm gonna build bridges a mile long. – George Bailey*

Play Video Session 1: Segment 1: George and Mary

George Bailey had big dreams and a detailed plan for his life. He knew exactly what he was going to do this year and in the years to come. As a boy, he dreamed of adventures on the South Sea that included harems and multiple wives. As a young adult, he desired to travel the world and build monumental bridges and skyscrapers.

But George was not just a dreamer; he was a doer. He had spent countless hours in the library researching and studying these places and saving his money to finance his adventures to vast lands.

The dominant factor surrounding George's dreams was his escape of what he considered the narrow constraints of Bedford Falls. He wanted freedom and adventure that he believed could not be found in the family business, the Bailey Building and Loan.

Likewise, we have dreams and plans for our lives. Some are idealistic and involve escaping the monotonous lives we have found ourselves in. Others are more ambitious and involve a lot of hard work now for an even larger payoff later.

It's good to make plans and have dreams. But what happens when those dreams and plans get delayed or, worse yet, never happen due to unforeseen circumstances? The fact is, life is full of interruptions that frustrate our plans. Health concerns, family crisis, expensive repairs, and job loss not only interrupt but often cancel our very important plans.

Perhaps it would do us good to look at these interruptions, delays, or even the cancellation of our plans as divine intervention. Some of the great advances in God's plans have come through "interruptions" to the normal routine. He often corrects our dreams and plans via struggles in life—some of which God orchestrates and others that He allows.

1. How would you react if your vacation plans got waylaid by a completely unforeseen and unexpected circumstance? Has something like this ever happened to you?

Very disappointed

Not that I recall

2. How would you describe George Bailey's plans for his life? What plans did you have for your life as a young high school or college student? How did those plans work out for you?

Architect, Travel

Teacher, not

Tragedies Interrupt Our Plans

DR. CAMPBELL: *They've appointed George here as executive secretary to take his father's place.*
GEORGE: *Oh, no! But, Uncle Billy...*
DR. CAMPBELL: *You can keep him on. That's all right. As secretary you can hire anyone you like.*
GEORGE: *Dr. Campbell, now let's get this thing straight. I'm leaving. I'm leaving right now. I'm going to school. This is my last chance. Uncle Billy here, he's your man.*
DR. CAMPBELL: *But, George, they'll vote with Potter otherwise.*

3. As a young man, what unexpected event happens that derails George's plans of leaving Bedford Falls to go to college, become an engineer, and then travel the world?

Father dies

Must run the Bldg + Loan

4. It has been said that we are either healing from a tragedy, suffering from a tragedy, or about to he broadsided by a tragedy. Share a time when a tragedy interrupted your plans.

5. Read Matthew 14:13–21. How does Jesus initially respond to the tragic death of John the Baptist? How do his plans for setting aside a time of mourning change? What blessing happens as a result?

6. If you had experienced a time of profound loss over a close friend, how might you have responded to seeing the crowd on the shore all vying for your attention?

7. How did George handle his life's tragedy and the interruption to his plans? What Christ-like action did George exhibit? Do you think he ever became jealous of his brother, Harry? Would you have? Explain.

People Interrupt Our Plans

GEORGE: *What's a pretty girl like you doing marrying this two-headed brother of mine?*

RUTH: *Well, I'll tell you. It's purely mercenary. My father offered him a job.*

HARRY: *George...about that job. Ruth spoke out of turn. I never said I'd take it. You've been holding the bag here for four years, and...well, I won't*

let you down, George. I would like to.... Oh, wait a minute. I forgot the bags.
I'll be right back.
***RUTH:** George, George, George...that's all Harry ever talks about.*
***GEORGE:** Ruth, this... what about this job?*
***RUTH:** Oh, well, my father owns a glass factory in Buffalo. He wants to get Harry started in the research business.*
***GEORGE:** Is it a good job?*
***RUTH:** Oh, yes, very. Not much money, but a good future, you know. Harry's a genius at research. My father fell in love with him.*
***GEORGE:** And you did, too?*

▌ Play Video Session 1: Segment 3: George Meets Ruth

8. As George grows four years older waiting for Harry to come back and take over the Building and Loan, what news does he receive that interrupts his plans once again to leave Bedford Falls? What sort of "mutual understanding" must he and Harry have had?

9. Read Matthew 26:26–46. When Jesus was overwhelmed with sorrow, he took Peter, James, and John with him into the Garden of Gethsemane. What did Jesus request of his friends? Was it a difficult request? How did they let him down?

10. Have you ever made great sacrifices for a family member or close friend only to be let down? How did you feel afterward? Did the relationship survive? If so, how? Why is this situation often much harder to handle than a business associate or an acquaintance letting you down?

11. Perhaps you have been betrayed in a friendship, or maybe you have even been the perpetrator and it cost you that relationship. What's so fascinating about Jesus's response to his friends when the mob came to arrest him? Do you think he was angry, upset, or disappointed?

12. How does George respond to this disappointing news? How do you think you would have handled the news?

MRS. THOMPSON: But my husband hasn't worked in over a year, and I need money.
WOMAN: How am I going to live until the bank opens?
MAN: I got doctor bills to pay.
MAN: I need cash.
MAN: Can't feed my kids on faith.
MARY: How much do you need?
GEORGE: Hey! I got two thousand dollars! Here's two thousand dollars. This'll tide us over until the bank reopens.

Play Video Session 1: Segment 4: George Saves the Day

13. What unexpected interruption in George's plans led to him saving the Building and Loan? What did he have to give up in order to do so?

14. What are some examples of interruptions in life that change our plans but are not the necessarily the result of evil or tragedy?

15. While witnessing the run on the bank from inside Ernie's cab, Mary urges George to leave town right away and to not go back to the Building and Loan. How do you know when an interruption deserves your attention or when it's best to disregard it? How do we know when an interruption is from God?

16. Read Luke 1:26–38. How might Joseph and Mary have felt when their lives were dramatically interrupted by an angelic announcement? What plans were interrupted? How might this interruption also have impacted those around them?

17. What did Mary and Joseph have to do in order to accept this interruption in their lives and move on? What did they gain from this interruption?

18. C.S. Lewis wrote to his close friend Arthur Greeves recommending that Christians stop regarding all the unpleasant things as interruptions of one's life. He wrote, "The great thing, if one can, is to stop regarding all the unpleasant things as interruptions of one's 'own,' or 'real' life. The truth is of course that what one calls the interruptions are precisely one's real life—the life God is sending one day by day." How might our outlook change if we start viewing life's interruptions not as obstacles to our plans but simply as the life God has sent us?

19. What was the result of George's selfless act of giving up his own money and honeymoon?

Evil Interrupts Our Plans

GEORGE: *I'm in trouble, Mr. Potter. I need help. Through some sort of an accident my company's short in their accounts. The bank examiner's up there today. I've got to raise eight thousand dollars immediately.*
POTTER: *Oh, so that's what the reporters wanted to talk to you about?*
GEORGE: *The reporters?*
POTTER: *Yes. They called me up from your Building and Loan. Oh, there's a man over there from the D.A.'s office, too. He's looking for you.*

GEORGE: *Please help me, Mr. Potter. Help me, won't you please? Can't you see what it means to my family? I'll pay you any sort of a bonus on the loan...any interest. If you still want the Building and Loan, why I...*
POTTER: *George, could it possibly be there's a slight discrepancy in the books?*
GEORGE: *No, sir. There's nothing wrong with the books. I've just misplaced eight thousand dollars. I can't find it anywhere.*
POTTER: *You misplaced eight thousand dollars?*
GEORGE: *Yes, sir.*

■ Play Video Session 1: Segment 5: George Begs Potter

20. What happens on Christmas Eve that interrupts George's plans of celebrating with his family? What could happen to George as a result?

21. Read Matthew 2:13–18. Why did Joseph move his family to Egypt? How would your plans suddenly change if God told you in the middle of the night to get up and move to a place you have never been?

22. What can we learn from this evil act committed by Herod regarding those who oppose God? How successful was Herod in his attempt to kill the Son of God? Read Romans 8:28.

23. Why does God allow evil to happen to those who are trying to do the right thing? Read Proverbs 3:5–6.

24. What good came out of the evil that was perpetrated in Bedford Falls? In what ways has George Bailey's life turned out differently than he had planned?

25. Popular culture tells us that the point of life is to be happy and that you must do everything you can to achieve this happiness or you will be bitter, frustrated, and full of regrets. How does *It's a Wonderful Life* fly in the face of that philosophy?

Session 2: People Were Human to Him

The sign on the wall in George Bailey's office reads, "All you take with you is that which you have given away." This aphorism epitomized George's life and is demonstrated most clearly when he gives his college money to his brother Harry so that he can go to school. Our lives are not measured in terms of how much money and fame we acquire but rather in that which we can give to our fellow man.

Valuing Others above Yourself

CLARENCE: *I know. I know. He didn't go.*
JOSEPH: *That's right. Not only that, but he gave his school money to his brother Harry, and sent him to college. Harry became a football star – made second team All American.*

■ Play Video Session 2: Segment 1: George Meets Potter

We can either treat people as objects, like Mr. Potter, or as God's creation with intrinsic value. The fact is, when we affirm and appreciate others, we raise their value. This is a fundamental truth found in Scripture: that each human life has value and that we are to love our neighbor as much as we do ourselves. So why is this so hard for us to put into practice?

We live in an age that caters to placing our own self-interests above those of others. We want the best seat, the most attention, and all our personal needs met to our satisfaction.

Putting others first involves risk and sacrifice. What will be asked of me? Will I have to give up my money or, worse yet, my time? Will it make me feel uncomfortable? Whom do I have to associate with? What if I do not like them or they do not like me? Valuing and loving everyone requires self-sacrifice and getting out of our comfort zones.

We do have a model in Jesus Christ because He loved all people. He loved thieves, prostitutes, tax collectors, diseased people, poor people, children, and his followers. He loved people who were devoted to him and those who were different from him. He even loved difficult and dangerous people.

This does not come naturally for us nor did it for George. He struggled with seeing Mr. Potter as anything but a "warped, frustrated old man." But overall, his selfless love for his friends, family, and community eventually won out.

Where do we begin this selfless journey? It all starts by seeing people as God sees them—as someone worth dying for. If God made them in His image and then sent his son to die for them, they have value, and that should matter to us.

1. Which of the following statements might be the most difficult for you to say?

    a) Go ahead. You can have the last piece of cake.
    b) Please go ahead of me in line. I'm in no hurry.
    c) I would love to use my free time helping clean the church.
    d) We're going to use our beach vacation money this year for an inner city ministry project.

You know, George, I feel that in a small way we are doing something important. Satisfying a fundamental urge. It's deep in the race for a man to want his own roof and walls and fireplace, and we're helping him get those things in our shabby little office.

– Peter Bailey

Play Video Session 2: Segment 2: George and His Pop

2. How would you describe George's father, Peter Bailey? How much influence do you think his actions had on George as a young man? Compare and contrast Peter Bailey and Mr. Potter.

3. If you were George and witnessed all your father had to go through, would you want to go into the family business? Did you ever consider going into the same occupation as one of your parents? Why or why not?

4. What is his father's response when George resists "being cooped up for the rest of [his] life in a shabby little office," complaining, "I'd go crazy. I want to do something big and something important?" How is George measuring success in life?

5. Read Matthew 13:31–32. What do you think Jesus is trying to say with the parable of the tiny mustard seed growing to become a great tree?

6. Why might we feel that the things that we do for others are insignificant in the grand scheme of life? What crucial role does our attitude play in helping others? According to James 3:5, what can one small spark do?

7. Do you think George understood the significance of his father's work at this time? Have you ever dismissed something as insignificant only to find out later that it was a significant blessing to others?

Valuing Others Involves Sacrifice

*Just a minute… just a minute. Now, hold on, Mr. Potter. You're right when you say my father was no businessman. I know that. Why he ever started this cheap, penny-ante Building and Loan, I'll never know. But neither you nor anyone else can say anything against his character, because his whole life was… why, in the 25 years since he and his brother, Uncle Billy, started this thing, he never once thought of himself. Isn't that right, Uncle Billy? He didn't save enough money to send Harry away to college, let alone me. But he did help a few people get out of your slums, Mr. Potter, and what's wrong with that? Why… here, you're all businessmen here. Doesn't it make them better citizens? Doesn't it make them better customers? You… you said… what'd you say a minute ago? They had to wait and save their money before they even ought to think of a decent home. Wait? Wait for what? Until their children grow up and leave them? Until they're so old and broken down that they… Do you know how long it takes a working man to save $5,000? Just remember this, Mr. Potter, that this rabble you're talking about… they do most of the working and paying and living and dying in this community. Well, is it too much to have them work and pay and live and die in a couple of decent rooms and a bath? Anyway, my father didn't think so. People were human beings to him. But to you, a warped, frustrated old man, they're cattle. Well in my book, my father died a much richer man than you'll ever be! – **George Bailey**

Play Video Session 2: Segment 3: George Defends His Father

8. When George's father suddenly dies, an incensed George comes to the defense of both his father and the institution he founded in a board meeting at the Building and Loan. What was George's rationale for why his father started the Building and Loan?

9. What sacrifices do you think Peter Bailey likely made while running the Building and Loan for twenty-five years? How do you know when a sacrifice is no longer worth it?

10. Read Matthew 19:16–22. What did the rich young ruler's response to Jesus indicate? Why is it so hard to sacrifice our wealth?

11. According to Matthew 10:38–39, what do you have to surrender and sacrifice to follow Christ?

12. Read Romans 12:1. How would you describe sacrificial living? Does it come naturally, or is it a choice? Explain.

13. How did Peter Bailey's sacrifices impact George's life and change an entire community? What did George have to sacrifice to follow in his father's footsteps?

Valuing the Significance of Others

He pulls some money from his pocket, and offers it to her.
VIOLET: *No, George, don't...*
GEORGE: *Here, now, you're broke, aren't you?*
VIOLET: *I know, but...*

GEORGE: What do you want to do, hock your furs, and that hat? Want to walk to New York? You know, they charge for meals and rent up there just the same as they do in Bedford Falls.

VIOLET: (taking money) Yeah – sure…

GEORGE: It's a loan. That's my business. Building and Loan. Besides, you'll get a job. Good luck to you.

VIOLET: I'm glad I know you, George Bailey.

Play Video Session 2: Segment 4: George and Violet

14. How would you describe Violet Bick? What do you think the community of Bedford Falls thinks of her? How does George treat her?

15. How does our cynicism about a person's reputation hinder us from helping them and then hinder them from making real change in their life? Why are we often hesitant to offer people second chances?

16. Read Luke 19:1–10. In Jewish culture, how would Zacchaeus being a tax collector have impacted his life? How would the average Jew see him? How did Jesus see him?

17. What does it say about Zacchaeus's awareness of his own need when he was not afraid to embarrass himself just to see Jesus?

18. What's significant about Jesus going to Zacchaeus's home, and how did the crowd respond?

19. What do Zacchaeus and the rich young ruler have in common? How are they different?

20. What is different about what Jesus asked the rich young ruler to do and what he asked of Zacchaeus? What did this show about the change in Zacchaeus?

21. Do you think most people would find it easier to associate with the rich young ruler or Zacchaeus? Why?

22. How can we be open and loving without being vulnerable and overly trusting? Where's the balance? How do we achieve this?

23. How does George's offer to give Violet a second chance help her maintain a sense of self-worth? In the end, what does she give back, and how might that have been a sacrifice for her?

Session 3: Bankruptcy, Scandal, and Prison

Bad decisions. We've all made them. Even in the most well-informed circumstances, we can, despite our best intentions, still choose poorly. There are other times when discontentment, stress, anger, and fear cloud our judgement and we ignore important information necessary to make a good choice.

Frustration Leads to Bad Decisions

---

*Where's that money, you stupid, silly old fool? Where's the money? Do you realize what this means? It means bankruptcy and scandal, and prison! That's what it means! One of us is going to jail! Well, it's not going to be me! – **George Bailey***

Play Video Session 3: Segment 1: George Kicks the Car

Just like us, George Bailey makes many decisions in his life, some more monumental than others. Some decisions he struggles with and makes the right choice—like turning down Mr. Potter's job offer after seeing through his scheme. Other times, George is consumed by his emotions and chooses poorly. And just like us, he has to live with the outcome.

Every decision we make bears a consequence that has the potential of changing the entire path of our lives—for good or bad. So it pays to consider your choices well. What outcome do you desire? Better decisions yield better outcomes. It's a simple truth.

Sometimes we might feel trapped or without options. But the truth is, there is always a better choice. Yes, some things might seem out of our control. But when we focus on what we can control, we'll be empowered by all the choices we really do have.

Eleanor Roosevelt said, "I am who I am today because of the choices I made yesterday." The fact is, we really are the sum of the choices we have made, big and small. All the more reason to keep our emotions intact, rely on good information, and then respond in a way that glorifies God and helps us to live with the outcome.

1. What is the worst decision you ever made? What led to you making that decision? What was the impact of that decision?

Discontent Leads to Bad Decisions

GEORGE: *Now what's your point, Mr. Potter?*
POTTER: *My point? My point is, I want to hire you.*
GEORGE: *Hire me?*
POTTER: *I want you to manage my affairs, run my properties. George, I'll start you out at twenty thousand dollars a year.*

GEORGE: Twenty thou… twenty thousand dollars a year?

POTTER: You wouldn't mind living in the nicest house in town, buying your wife a lot of fine clothes, a couple of business trips to New York a year, maybe once in a while Europe. You wouldn't mind that, would you, George?

GEORGE: Would I?

A little later…

GEORGE: No…no…no…no, now wait a minute, here! I don't have to talk to anybody! I know right now, and the answer is no! NO! Doggone it! You sit around here and you spin your little webs and you think the whole world revolves around you and your money. Well, it doesn't, Mr. Potter! In the… in the whole vast configuration of things, I'd say you were nothing but a scurvy little spider.

▄▄ Play Video Session 3: Segment 2: George Faces Temptation

2. Why might George have been unhappy or discontent with his current status in life?

3. In the 1930s the average annual household income was $1,970.00. George was making approximately $2,340 ($45 x 52 weeks). Mr. Potter's offer would multiply his salary almost by a factor of ten. Think about your current salary and then multiply it by a factor of ten. How would you respond if you were suddenly offered a job making ten times your current salary? What in your life would change?

4. Why did George turn down Potter's offer, and how hard do you think that was? How hard would it be for you to turn down an offer making ten times your salary if it meant compromising your beliefs?

5. How would you define contentment? What does our contentment have to do with our happiness? How has your contentment level changed as you have aged?

6. According to Paul in Philippians 4:11–13, what's the secret to being content? Why is contentment a process that we must learn and work at?

7. What does Jesus say is essential to learning contentment in Matthew 6:33? Does seeking first God's kingdom and righteousness mean we all should become full-time missionaries?

8. Do you think George made a good or bad decision by turning Mr. Potter down? How might his life have been different had he not turned Potter down?

Anger Leads to Bad Decisions

GEORGE: Is that Zuzu's teacher?
MARY: Yes.
GEORGE: Let me speak to her.
GEORGE: Hello. Hello, Mrs. Welch? This is George Bailey. I'm Zuzu's father. Say, what kind of a teacher are you anyway? What do you mean sending her home like that, half naked? Do you realize she'll probably end up with pneumonia on account of you?
MARY: George!
GEORGE: Is this the sort of thing we pay taxes for—to have teachers like

you? Silly, stupid, careless people who send our kids home without any
clothes on? You know, maybe my kids aren't the best-dressed kids; maybe
they don't have any decent clothes…

◢ Play Video Session 3: Segment 3: George gets Angry

9. In what ways might George's anger and frustration with Uncle Billy, Zuzu's teacher, and Mary and the kids have worsened an already bad situation?

10. The problem with anger is that if it is left unchecked, it can lead to us hurting others around us. How do you keep your anger from hurting those around you?

11. What is James's instruction for us regarding our anger in James 1:19–20? What do the following verses say about why we should control our anger?

Psalm 86:15 –

Proverbs 10:19 –

Proverbs 13:3 –

Proverbs 14:29 –

12. How does the emergence of instant communication in today's modern culture present a challenge to managing anger? What might George have done if he had access to email, texting, or social media?

13. According to Ephesians 4:26 is it a sin to be angry? In Mark 3:5 and Matthew 21:12–13 where was Jesus's anger ultimately directed?

14. How might George have responded differently in his anger with Zuzu's teacher, Mary and the kids, and Uncle Billy?

*Look at you. You used to be so cocky! You were going to go out and conquer the world! You once called me a warped, frustrated old man. What are you but a warped, frustrated young man? A miserable little clerk crawling in here on your hands and knees and begging for help. No securities—no stocks—no bonds—nothing but a miserable little five hundred dollar equity in a life insurance policy. You're worth more dead than alive. – **Potter***

Play Video Session 3: Segment 4: George Prays

15. Why does George Bailey feel hopeless enough to consider suicide? How does his financial crisis quickly become a crisis of faith?

16. Recent data reveals that suicide rates have increased dramatically over the last 50 years in all states. What causes people to lose hope today to the point that they would consider ending their life?

17. George is terrified of his future. And even though he is not a praying man, he turns to the Lord in a simple yet honest prayer. Moments later, George is punched in the face, wrecks his car, and is left stranded in the snow. He feels like there's no hope at all and that the world would be better off without him in it. Have you ever felt like things just got worse the more you prayed? Why would God allow that when we are sincerely seeking Him in prayer?

18. Jimmy Stewart once said regarding his prayer in the movie, "In agony I raise my eyes and, following the script, plead, 'God… God… dear Father in heaven, I'm not a praying man, but if you're up there and you can hear me, show me the way. I'm at the end of my rope. Show me the way, God….' As I said those words, I felt the loneliness, the hopelessness of people who had nowhere to turn, and my eyes filled with tears. I broke down sobbing. This was not planned at all, but the power of that prayer, the realization that our Father in heaven is there to help the hopeless, had reduced me to tears." Have you ever been in prayer and then suddenly felt the magnitude of what you were praying for? Explain.

19. Read Romans 4:18–25. How did Abraham maintain hope when all the facts pointed to something else?

20. Was Abraham just denying reality, a dreamer holding on to some romantic notion of having children one day? Do we have to ignore the facts in order to have faith?

21. How should we respond when the facts before us are the opposite of what God has promised?

22. Read 2 Corinthians 5:7 and Hebrews 11:1. What does it mean to walk by faith, not by sight?

23. George chose to cling to the facts before him rather than place his hope and trust in a God who could answer his prayer and save him. How about you? What are you trusting God to do that He told you He would do? Where is your day-to-day faith application?

Session 4: George, It's a Miracle! It's a Miracle!

A 2013 Harris Poll found that 72% of people believe in miracles, yet out of that same group, only 57% believe in the virgin birth. A further dive into this survey might have also indicated that miracles are important when we need one but a little harder to believe when someone else does.

But isn't divine intervention what separates Christianity from every other religion? The entire Christian faith is based around a divine act orchestrated by a supreme God to save all humanity from their sins. Sounds like a miracle to me!

God Intervenes with Miracles

Come on in here now. Now, you stand right over here, by the tree. Right there, and don't move, don't move. I hear 'em now, George, it's a miracle! It's a miracle! – **Mary**

🎬 **Play Video Session 4: Segment 1: George Gets a Miracle**

The main storyline of *It's a Wonderful Life* is supported by a divine act. In fact, the first scene in the movie finds the community of Bedford Falls petitioning God to save a fledgling George Bailey.

George, though not a praying man, also finds himself calling out for proof that God is alive and active in the world—and, if God is there, to provide him direction.

The prophet Isaiah proclaimed, "The virgin will conceive and give birth to a son, and they will call him Immanuel" (which means "God is with us") (Isaiah 7:14). The miracle of Jesus Christ's birth announced to the world that God is with us! He acts and intercedes on our behalf, which is exactly what George would find out later in the movie—that God was with him.

Why do we, then, intentionally separate ourselves from a God who desires to be with us? We place limitations on God's power and doubt that He can come through in our moment of crisis.

We serve a God who has unlimited power to act on our behalf when called upon. What if we began to truly believe this by putting his kingdom first and expecting miracles? What sort of miracles would we be witnessing and participating in every day? The fact is, life is wonderful because God intervenes!

1. Have you been witness to what you would consider a miracle? If so, explain.

MR. GOWER: *I owe everything to George Bailey. Help him, dear Father.*
MR. MARTINI: *Joseph, Jesus and Mary. Help my friend Mr. Bailey.*
MRS. BAILEY: *Help my son George tonight.*
BERT THE COP: *He never thinks about himself, God; that's why he's in trouble.*
ERNIE THE CAB DRIVER: *George is a good guy. Give him a break, God.*
MARY: *I love him, dear Lord. Watch over him tonight.*
JANIE: *Please, God. Something's the matter with Daddy.*
ZUZU: *Please bring Daddy back.*

Play Video Session 4: Segment 2: George is Prayed For

2. What motivated the community of Bedford Falls to begin praying for George in the opening scenes of the movie? What did their prayers motivate them to do?

3. What motivates you to bring your friends and family before God in prayer? Are your prayers stand-alone events, or do they move you to action?

4. According to Luke 5:17–26, what motivated the men to get their paralytic friend to Jesus? What obstacles did they encounter? Did the men ever give up?

5. What sort of obstacles do you encounter while praying for others? How do you get more focused prayer time?

6. Whose faith was demonstrated in this story, the man or his friends? What was the difference between the friends' faith and the crowd that was there?

7. What vital role did this man's friends play in the miracle that he experienced? How does your faith benefit your friends and family and vice versa?

8. What expectations do you think the paralytic had from his friends' actions? Why did Jesus also forgive his sin, and what was this man's sin? Was his physical or spiritual healing more important?

9. In addition to saving him from financial ruin, what more important miracle did God perform for George Bailey?

10. Have you ever thought that maybe you could be someone's miracle? Are we willing to take that risk and do something that might seem awkward, strange, or risky?

God Intervenes When We Pray

God... God... Dear Father in Heaven, I'm not a praying man, but if you're up there and you can hear me, show me the way. I'm at the end of my rope. Show me the way, God. – George

Play Video Session 4: Segment 3: George Prays

11. George tells God, "I'm not a praying man." How would you describe George Bailey's prayer? Do you think it was difficult for George to pray in light of the fact that he was not a "praying man"? Why or why not?

12. Do you find it difficult to pray in private, in public, or both? Explain. Did someone teach you to pray, or did you just begin praying?

13. Read Matthew 6:5–8. Have you seen people pray like those described in this passage? How did it make you feel? What does Jesus say their reward will be?

14. According to verse 8, God knows what we need before we even ask. If this is true, why should we pray? Wouldn't this qualify as meaningless repetition or babbling?

15. George referred to God as "Father." Consider the phrase "Our Father." What does this phrase communicate to you, and how does it make you feel? What pictures does it bring to mind? In what ways is God like a father?

16. In Mark 14:36, Romans 8:15, and Galatians 4:6, a more intimate term is used for God. It is the Aramaic word "Abba," which would most closely be translated as "Daddy." How does this change the meaning of your prayers? Do you always pray using the same name for God, or do you use different names?

17. What does George Baily teach us about prayer?

God Intervenes at the Right Time

CLARENCE: *Your lip's bleeding, George.*
GEORGE: *Yeah, I got a bust in the jaw in answer to a prayer a little bit ago.*
CLARENCE: *Oh, no – no – no. I'm the answer to your prayer. That's why I was sent down here.*

18. What is Clarence's job regarding George Bailey? How does George accept Clarence's intervention in his life? Does he see Clarence as the answer to his prayer?

19. That word "intervention" conveys the idea that the existing situation before the intervention was wrong or harmful in some way. How did God intervene in human history in Luke 2:1–20? Why did God intervene according to Matthew 20:28?

20. Was the birth of a baby boy, found lying in a manger, with common parents the answer to prayer that most people thought they needed? Why should we not underestimate the package that God sends his miracles in?

21. What are some ways in which God continues to intervene in the world today?

22. What do Clarence and Hebrews 13:2 teach us about God answering our prayers and miracles?

Session 5: You've Been Given a Great Gift, George.

One of the reasons *It's a Wonderful Life* makes such an excellent Bible study is that it emphasizes the importance of every life. Regardless of your gender, race, talents, abilities, or socioeconomic status, your life has value and matters.

Every Life Is a Gift

You've been given a great gift, George. A chance to see what the world would be like without you. – ***Clarence***

 Play Video Session 5: Segment 1: George Gets a Gift

George Bailey believes he has never accomplished anything really useful or interesting in life. He is stuck in the same dull work, day after day—a far cry from the adventurous life he imagined as a young man, traveling the world and building monumental skyscrapers and bridges.

This disappointment, combined with his current crisis, leads him to wonder whether everyone would be better off without him or, better yet, if he had never been born.

Have you ever felt this way? Have your youthful dreams vanished, leaving you feeling trapped in a life that's not at all what you expected? Do you find yourself asking, "What's the point? Am I making any impact on the world around me? Who benefits from my existence?"

The fact is, the Bible says God "formed you in the womb" and "knows the plans that he has for you." So according to the creator of the universe, your life has value! This is true regardless of your gender, race, physical or mental attributes or abilities, occupation, financial status, or residence.

The reason we are so easily distracted from this truth is that we buy into the lie that there's a better life just beyond our grasp. As a result, we become discontent with the cards we've been dealt, and when crisis comes, we're unable to manage our emotions and reactions that come with it.

George Bailey's opportunity to see a world without him in it reminds us of what is truly meaningful in life. The truth is that George's life was not wasted but rather everyone would have suffered terribly had he not been born. The same can be said for us. Even though we are not granted the same opportunity as George—to see a world without us—we can trust that the God who gave us life has a purpose and plan for it.

1. If you had the opportunity to see what the world would be like had you never been born, would you? If so, why?

CLARENCE: *Hmmm, this isn't going to be so easy. So you still think killing yourself would make everyone feel happier, eh?*

GEORGE: *Oh, I don't know. I guess you're right. I suppose it would have been better if I'd never been born at all.*

2. Why does George think everyone would be much better off had he never been born? Even before Clarence's vision of a world without him, what or who is he failing to consider at that moment with that request?

3. If given the opportunity, what questions might George have wanted to ask God about the state of his life thus far?

4. When in the midst of tragedy or crisis, what questions might we ask God? What happens when no answer is immediately given?

5. Read Job 3:1–3, 11–12, 16, 20–23, 25–26. Following a seven-day period of silence and because of the degree of his suffering, Job comes very close to cursing God but never does. What does he do instead and why?

6. After cursing the day he was born, what does Job begin to do next in verses 11 and 12?

7. How are George and Job alike? Why is unexplained trouble so hard for us to bear?

8. Job's story, like George's, doesn't end in his crisis. Read Job 42:12. What transformation happens in Job's life that should give us hope when we're experiencing difficult times?

9. Had George mediated on Jeremiah 29:11 during his crisis, how might his desire to see a world without his existence been different?

Every Life Impacts Others

GEORGE: *That's a lie! Harry Bailey went to war! He got the Congressional Medal of Honor! He saved the lives of every man on that transport.*
CLARENCE: *Every man on that transport died. Harry wasn't there to save them because you weren't there to save Harry. You see, George, you really had a wonderful life. Don't you see what a mistake it would be to throw it away?*

Play Video Session 5: Segment 2: George at the Cemetery

10. Responding to George's wish to have never been born, what sort of nightmare scene does Clarence unveil? What impact did George's absence have far beyond that of Bedford Falls?

11. How does this dramatic episode that George experiences speak to the choices we make each day in our own lives?

12. Over 200 years ago, Edmund Burke wrote to Thomas Mercer, "The only thing necessary for the triumph of evil is for good men to do nothing." How is this statement true when you consider the dark alternate reality of Pottersville?

13. Read Matthew 25:14–26. Why do you think the master gives the men different amounts of compensation?

14. What valuable gifts does God provide us today, and how does he expect those gifts to be invested?

15. If the master received back what He gave the servant, why is he so upset? Should he not be grateful that he at least had his original investment back?

16. Read Luke 12:48. What type of return on investment does God expect from the gifts we receive?

17. What causes us to be fearful about using our gifts, talents, and abilities? What happens when we don't use the gifts, talents, and abilities that God has given us?

18. What did the vision of Pottersville show George about the gifts, talents, and abilities he was given?

Every Life Is to Be Enjoyed

"Dear George, remember no man is a failure who has friends. Thanks for the wings, Love Clarence."

▶ Play Video Session 5: Segment 3: George's Wonderful Life

19. What does George finally learn about his life when the town comes to his rescue on Christmas Eve? What does this understanding compel him to do?

20. After George races home, what little things does he appreciate that he had thoughtlessly ignored before?

21. How does learning to appreciate the small things in life help us appreciate and value our lives as a whole? What are some of those small things in life that you have learned to value over the years? When we neglect to enjoy these little things, what are we left with in life?

22. Read Ecclesiastes 2:24, 3:12–13, 5:18, 8:15, 9:9, and 11:9. What is Solomon teaching us in these verses? Is Solomon preaching hedonism; the pursuit of pleasure and sensual self-indulgence; to eat, drink, and be merry all the time because we will soon die?

23. How does Solomon balance his previous statements about enjoying life with Ecclesiastes 12:13–14?

24. How is Harry's description of George as the richest man in town now accurate?

25. George found out that he truly had a wonderful life. Take some time to write out why your life is wonderful and why you should be thankful to God for it.

Movie Production

Although a seasonal classic today, *It's a Wonderful Life* was a flop at the box office when it was released in 1946, despite the presence of one of the era's most bankable stars, Jimmy Stewart. Today it's now generally thought to be one of the greatest American movies ever made, by the American Film Institute.

Although most people know *It's a Wonderful Life* from the Capra film, the story of George Bailey was first told in a short story titled *The Greatest Gift*, by Philip Van Doren Stern. Stern wrote the short story in 1943 after working on it for several years. After failing to get it published, he sent 200 copies to his friends as Christmas cards.

One of those Christmas cards landed on the desk of RKO Pictures producer, David Hempstead. He subsequently purchased the motion picture rights to the story for $10,000 with hopes of turning it into a movie starring Cary Grant. After RKO was unable to produce a suitable script, Grant went on to make another holiday classic, *The Bishop's Wife*.

In 1944 the rights were sold to director Frank Capra's production company, Liberty Films. Capra was the quintessential maker of movies of hope, which is why his movies often get labeled as "Capra corn" for the sweet sentimentality found in them. Capra immediately saw this story's potential, and after several screenplay revisions, Capra renamed it *It's a Wonderful Life*.

Capra pitched the movie idea to Jimmy Stewart about an extraordinary but deeply discouraged man who, around Christmas, is allowed to see what the world would have been like had he never been born. Stewart almost didn't take the job, but after many negotiations and much encouragement from Lionel Barrymore, who played Mr. Potter, Stewart was convinced to take the role.

Even though it did not meet box office expectations, the picture did garner five Academy Award nominations: Best Picture, Best Actor, Best Director, Best Sound Recording, and Best Film Editing. Despite being nominated, it won no Oscars but was beat out by the award-winning *The Best Years of Our Lives*.

During the 1970s, after a clerical error prevented the copyright from being renewed properly, the film entered public domain and was shown continually on cable channels the weeks leading up to Christmas as well as being sold royalty free on VHS.

In the 1990s, the courts found that even though the film's images had entered public domain, the film's story was protected by virtue of it being a derivative work of *The Greatest Gift*, whose copyright was properly renewed by RKO in 1971. Today, NBC is licensed to show the film on U.S. network television and traditionally shows it twice during the Christmas season.

Seventy years later, *It's a Wonderful Life* has become a premier classic and favorite Christmas movie. Capra revealed that the film was his personal favorite among those he directed, adding that he screened it for his family every Christmas season. Stewart also reportedly considered it to be one of his favorite films that he had acted in.

Fun Facts

If you are a fan of *It's a Wonderful Life* like me, you will enjoy these 60 fun facts that I found while conducting research for the Bible study.

1. *It's a Wonderful Life* is based on the short story, *The Greatest Gift*, by Philip Van Doren Stern.
2. Stern was unable to get the story published and instead printed up 200 copies for his friends as Christmas cards. David Hempstead, a producer at RKO Pictures, got one and purchased the movie rights for $10,000.
3. Hempstead's plans involved Cary Grant in the lead as George Bailey, but after unsuccessfully producing a suitable script, the movie rights were sold to Frank Capra.
4. The movie is ranked as the #1 Most Inspirational Movie of All Time by the American Film Institute (2006).
5. Capra did not pitch the movie well to Stewart. Stewart later recalled replying, "Frank, if you want me to be in a picture about a guy that wants to kill himself and an angel comes down named Clarence who can't swim and I save him, when do we start?"
6. Lionel Barrymore convinced James Stewart to take the role of George, despite his feeling that he was not up to it so soon after World War II.
7. Although she had appeared in other movies, the movie marked Donna Reed's first starring role.
8. Donna Reed actually threw the rock that broke the window in the old Grandville house herself. Capra had hired a marksman to shoot it out for her on cue had she missed.

9. Other actresses considered for the role of Mary Bailey were Olivia de Havilland, Martha Scott, Ann Dvorak, and Ginger Rogers.

10. Beulah Bondi, who plays Mrs. Bailey, had previously played Jimmy Stewart's mother in *Mr. Smith Goes to Washington, Of Human Hearts*, and *Vivacious Lady*.

11. Capra, Reed, and Stewart have all cited *It's a Wonderful Life* as their favorite movie.

12. At $3.7 million, this was a very expensive independent production. In its initial box office run, it only earned $3.3 million.

13. The movie was not an immediate hit with audiences. In fact, it put Capra $525,000 in the hole, which left him scrambling to finance his production company's next picture, *State of the Union*.

14. The movie's copyright lapsed in 1974, making it available royalty free to anyone who wanted to show it for the next 20 years.

15. In the 1990s, the courts found that even though the film's images had entered public domain, the film's story was protected by virtue of it being a derivative work of *The Greatest Gift*, whose copyright was properly renewed by Stern in 1971.

16. Over time the movie has racked up about $70 million in DVD and merchandise sales.

17. The set for Bedford Falls was constructed in two months on four acres at RKO's Encino Ranch. It was one of the most elaborate movie sets ever built up to that time, with 75 stores and buildings, 20 fully grown oak trees, factories, residential areas, and a 300-yard-long Main Street—three whole city blocks.

18. Capra estimated the film would be shot within 90 days; he was right, and the whole cast and crew threw a party to celebrate.

19. Although Bedford Falls is a fictitious place, the town of Seneca Falls, New York, is said to be the real-life inspiration for the town as Frank Capra visited the town prior to making the movie.

20. The swimming pool under the gymnasium floor really exists at Beverly Hills High School and is still being used today.

21. Carl Switzer, a.k.a. Alfalfa of *The Little Rascals*, is who pushes the button that opens the dance floor over the swimming pool.

22. Lionel Barrymore (Mr. Potter) bet Donna Reed, a former farm girl from Iowa, $50 that she could not milk a cow on the set. She won the bet.

23. Despite the snowy look of Bedford Falls, the movie was shot in the summer of 1946—in the midst of a heat wave.

24. Previous films had used cornflakes painted white to portray snow, but Capra engineered a new technique for making snow by using a mixture of fomite (found in fire extinguishers), sugar, and water to create a quieter option. They used 6,000 gallons of the fake snow for filming and the Motion Picture Academy gave a special award to the RKO effects department for developing this new technique.

25. Karolyn Grimes, who played Zuzu in the film, didn't see the film until 1980.

26. In 1947 the FBI issued a memo noting the film as a potential "Communist infiltration of the motion picture industry," citing its "rather obvious attempts to discredit bankers by casting Lionel Barrymore as a 'Scrooge-type'" so that he would be the most hated man in the picture.

27. The rumor that Bert the cop and Ernie the cab driver were the inspiration for *Sesame Street*'s Bert and Ernie are false, according to Jerry Juhl, head writer for *The Muppet Show* and Jim Henson's longtime collaborator.

28. Mr. Potter's full name is Henry F. Potter, as written on the door of his office.

29. When Uncle Billy, Thomas Mitchell, gets drunk at Harry's wedding party and staggers off scene, the loud crash that is heard is actually someone knocking over some props during filming. Mitchell's quick impromptu saved the scene when he quipped, "I'm all right! I'm all right!" Capra decided to use this take in the final cut and gave the clumsy stagehand a $10 bonus for "improving the sound."

30. When George is running down Main Street, the movie marquee proclaims that it's showing *The Bells of St. Mary*, which was coincidentally a film Henry Travers, a.k.a. Clarence, also starred in.

31. In the scene in the bar when George breaks down, viewers are actually watching Stewart break into tears as he was so overcome with emotion that he began to sob right then and there.

32. Having just been away to war, Stewart was uncomfortable with performing the kiss scene with Donna Reed and put it off for weeks. The scene turned out to be one of the best in the film, and part of it even had to be cut to get past the censors.

33. A photograph of James Stewart at the age of six months, donated by his parents, was included in the Bailey home set.

34. Capra's first script included an alternate ending with George falling to his knees and reciting the Lord's Prayer.

35. George hopes to go to college to "learn how to build things." In real life, James Stewart majored in architecture at Princeton University.

36. In the version of this film that aired on TV in the late 1950s and early 1960s, George's line to Zuzu's teacher on the phone, "What do you mean, sending her home like that half naked?", was replaced with an alternate take in which he says, "What do you mean, sending my kid home from school in the rain?"

37. The name Zuzu comes from Zu Zu Ginger Snaps. George makes reference to this near the end of the movie when he says to Zuzu at the top of the stairs, "Zuzu, my little Ginger Snap!"

38. Sheldon Leonard, who played Nick the bartender, became the famed producer of *Make Room for Daddy* (1953), *Gomer Pyle: USMC* (1964), *The Dick Van Dyke Show* (1961), *The Andy Griffith Show* (1960), and *I Spy* (1965).

39. The original script ended with "Ode to Joy," not "Auld Lang Syne."

40. The story spans 26 years, from 1919 to 1945.

41. During the bank run scene, Ellen Corby, who later played Grandma Walton in *The Waltons*, went off script with her request for $17.50, which caught Stewart off-guard, and he kissed her, which was not in the script.

42. One of the film's posters shows an illustrated George holding Mary in the air, but this scene never appears in the film.

43. Vincent Price was considered for the part of Mr. Potter.

44. There are several examples of product placement in Gower's drugstore: Coca-Cola, Paterson tobacco pipes, La Unica cigars, Camel cigarettes, Lucky Strike cigarettes, Chesterfield cigarettes, Sweet Caporal cigarettes, Vaseline hair tonic, Penetro cough syrup, Pepto-Bismol, Bayer Aspirin, and *The Saturday Evening Post*.

45. Just as Alfred Hitchcock was famous for making on-screen cameos in all of his movies, Uncle Billy's pet raven, Jimmy, can be found in every Frank Capra production since 1938's *You Can't Take It With You.*

46. "Buffalo Gals" plays seven times throughout the film.

47. May 3, 1919, is the date of the telegram Mr. Gower receives notifying him of his son's death. However, the wall calendar outside Peter Bailey's office is set to June.

48. George smokes a cigarette, a cigar, and a pipe in the film.

49. Sam Wainright's catchphrase, "hee-haw" is said 13 times throughout the movie and not always by him.

50. Clarence Odbody was born in May 1693.

51. Violet is the only character to call George Georgy or Georgy Porgy.

52. In the original script, Clarence was to confront Potter about what he did to George. It was to take place right after Potter yelled, "And Happy New Year to you, in jail!"

53. The framed picture on George's office wall underneath his deceased father reads, "All you take with you is that which you given away."

54. Although Violet catches Mary's bouquet, she never marries.

55. In the original script, the boys weren't sledding when young George saved his brother from drowning—they were playing hockey on Mr. Potter's property. In that version of the story, George rescues Harry after Mr. Potter sets loose a pack of vicious dogs to chase the boys off his property.

56. George Bailey ranks No. 9 on the American Film Institute's list of the 100 greatest heroes in movie history. As for the greatest movie villains, Mr. Potter is No. 6.

57. Carol Coombs got the part of Janie Bailey because the casting director thought she looked like Donna Reed.

58. In a scene near the end of the movie, George enters the Building and Loan with a Christmas wreath on his arm. On hearing that he has a phone call from his brother Harry, he tosses the wreath on a table and picks up the phone. A second later, the wreath is back on his arm.

59. Harry Bailey's tombstone has the dates of 1911 and 1919 making him at most eight years old when he died, but the angel states that Harry died when he was nine.

60. The film has two lines of "secret dialogue" spoken quietly through Peter Bailey's office door. After a young George takes up for his father after Potter's insult and is ushered out of the room, George overhears through the glass pane of the door the following: POTTER: What's the answer? PETER BAILEY: Potter, you just humiliated me in front of my son.

Leave us a Review

Thank you again for doing this Bible study! I hope and pray that in some way it encouraged you (and your group) to grow closer to Christ this Christmas season.

If you enjoyed this study we would appreciate your leaving us an honest review on Amazon! Your review will help others know if this study is right for them and their small group.

It's easy and will only take a minute. Just search for "It's a Wonderful Life Study Guide" on Amazon. Click on the product in the search results and then click on reviews.

Thank you and God Bless!

Alan

Other Studies from Brown Chair Books

On the following pages you'll find the Introduction and a Chapter Sample from some of our other Bible Studies.

www.BrownChairBooks.com

A CHRISTMAS CAROL STUDY GUIDE
Book and Bible Study Based on A *Christmas Carol*
By Alan Vermilye

A Christmas Carol Book and Bible Study Guide includes the entire book of this Dickens classic as well as Bible study discussion questions for each chapter, Scripture references, and related commentary.

Detailed character sketches and an easy-to-read book summary provide deep insights into each character while examining the book's themes of greed, isolation, guilt, blame, compassion, generosity, transformation, forgiveness, and finally redemption. To help with those more difficult discussion questions, a complete Answer Guide is available for free online.

What others are saying:

The study is perfect for this time of the year turning our focus to the reason for the season - Jesus - and the gift of redemption we have through him. - Connie

I used this for an adult Sunday School class. We all loved it! – John

This study is wonderful! – Lori

I found this a refreshing look at the Bible through the eyes of Ebenezer Scrooch's life. – Lynelle

A CHRISTMAS CAROL STUDY GUIDE
INTRODUCTION

A CHRISTMAS CAROL by Charles Dickens has always been a favorite of mine. However, I must confess that it is not through Dickens's novel that I was first exposed to this classic piece of literature. No, I, like probably many of you, followed Ebenezer Scrooge through classic movies, television shows, plays, and, yes, Scrooge McDuck. In fact, it was not until recently that I read the book in preparation for this study. I'm so glad I did!

Many of Dickens's other novels and short stories made their way into my formative years' reading, including *Great Expectations* and *David Copperfield*. *A Christmas Carol*, unfortunately, was never "required reading" in school. Too bad…it should have been.

It's amazing how one book's vernacular has become commonplace during the holiday season. We're accused of being a "Scrooge" if we lack yuletide cheer, and we have fun reciting Tiny Tim's charge, "God bless us every one." And who of us has not uttered the occasional "Bah Humbug!" when standing in long checkout lines during the holidays?

Dickens wrote the novel both because he needed money at the time and to dictate a powerful social message that he wished to convey. Now, over 160 years later, this message is still being played out in movies, commercials, greeting cards, and our own subconscious, where we, too, challenge ourselves to be full of the "Christmas spirit," as Scrooge was that Christmas morning. It is possible that no other single piece of fiction has had the kind of sweeping cultural influence that can be attributed to Charles Dickens's first Christmas story.

In addition to the Christmas spirit, there are many themes that run deep through this book, most notably the themes of redemption and free will. It is fascinating to watch Scrooge's transformation from a mean, penny-pinching miser to a loving, generous benefactor. Scrooge has the wonderful and frightening opportunity to see visions of the future where he is told of things that "may" be, not what "will" be. He has the power to change the future with his present actions…and so do we!

Scrooge's transformation was life altering and not limited to the Christmas season. It was permanent. Each day after, he desired to be a better man for himself and his fellow man.

If you, too, had the opportunity to see how your present actions would impact the future, what would you change?

One action I thought I would take is to write this study. I'm not an expert on Dickens's literature nor a biblical scholar, but I do enjoy writing studies. I hope that reading this classic novel, watching one of the many movies, and thinking through the corresponding study questions will draw you closer to the only one who can provide lasting transformation—Jesus Christ.

A CHRISTMAS CAROL STUDY GUIDE
CHAPTER 1 SAMPLE

THE MAIN THEME found in *A Christmas Carol* is the celebration of Christmas and the good it inspires. However, Dickens weaves many themes throughout the pages of his classic novel, including traditions, Christmas spirit, family, social injustice, greed, generosity, forgiveness, the threat of time, and, most importantly, redemption and free will. Regardless of where you are in life, one of these themes will most likely resonate with you.

Icebreaker:

What is your favorite Christmas tradition and why?

Discussion Questions

1. When you hear the word Scrooge today, what comes to mind? What type of person exemplifies the typical Scrooge today? How do you handle the Scrooges in your life?

2. When you hear the words bah humbug, what comes to mind? Have you ever felt like uttering those or similar words during the Christmas season? Why?

3. If someone were to ask you, "What is Christmas spirit?" how would you answer? For some, why does the Christmas season bring out a desire to want to help the less fortunate?

4. When asked to make a Christmas donation to the poor, Scrooge adamantly refuses in favor of government institutions that he supports for that endeavor. The three institutions that Scrooge supported were the workhouses, the prisons, and the treadmill. Do some research, and describe those institutions and the Poor Laws that enabled them during 19th century Victorian England.

5. To understand why Charles Dickens wrote *A Christmas Carol*, we need to look no further than the person of Ebenezer Scrooge. How might Dickens's father being sentenced to a debtor's prison when Charles was just twelve years old have impacted his writings on this subject?

6. Scrooge stereotyped the poor and needy as "idle." What are some stereotypes that we might harbor about the poor or needy today? Do you think that most people consider it the government's responsibility to provide for the needy? Why do you think many people might have become hardened or cynical to the poor and needy?

7. Read Proverbs 14:31, 22:9, and 28:27 and Matthew 19:21. What do these passages say about serving the poor and needy among you? According to these verses, what happens when we help the poor? Whose job does Scripture say it is to take care of the poor—the government or the people?

8. Why might we sometimes avoid helping others less fortunate? How do the following passages tell us to respond to the poor that might also

be someone we dislike or an enemy? Read 1 John 3:17, Luke 6:35, and Romans 12:20.

9. The Bible commands that we be generous and that we help those in need (especially our Christian brothers and sisters). How do we know when we are being taken advantage of? Read 2 Thessalonians 3:10.

10. The concept of time is a theme that runs throughout the book. Scrooge is haunted by the ghosts of the past, present, and future. There are bells chiming and clocks tolling, reminding Scrooge of time passing. The chain that Marley bears reminds Scrooge of an endless prison sentence. Read Psalm 39:4–5 and James 4:13–17. What do these verses say about how we should manage our time here on this earth?

11. Through the story, we witness Scrooge's transformation from a mean, penny-pinching miser to a generous benefactor. His transformation and redemption are made possible through his free will. If you had the opportunity to see a vision of the future based on the choices you are making now, would you do it? Why or why not? How might it impact how you are living right now?

MERE CHRISTIANITY STUDY GUIDE
A Bible Study on the C.S. Lewis Book *Mere Christianity*
By Steven Urban

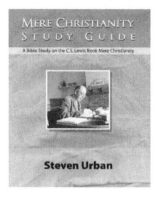

Mere Christianity Study Guide takes participants through a study of C.S. Lewis's classic *Mere Christianity*. Yet despite its recognition as a "classic," there is surprisingly little available today in terms of a serious study course.

This 12-week Bible study digs deep into each chapter and, in turn, into Lewis's thoughts. Perfect for small group sessions, this interactive workbook includes daily, individual study as well as a complete appendix and commentary to supplement and further clarify certain topics. Multiple week format options are also included.

What others are saying:

This study guide is more than just a guide to C.S Lewis' Mere Christianity, it is a guide to Christianity itself. – Crystal

Wow! What a lot of insight and food for thought! Perfect supplement to Mere Christianity. I think Mr. Lewis himself would approve. – Laurie

Our group is in the middle of studying Mere Christianity and I have found this guide to be invaluable.
– Angela

This is a very useful and comprehensive guide to Mere Christianity. – John

MERE CHRISTIANITY STUDY GUIDE
FOREWARD

During World War II, C. S. Lewis delivered a series of radio broadcasts on the BBC in England. At the time of the broadcasts the outcome of the war was still very uncertain. People needed hope. Many tuned in to see what this Oxford scholar might have to say. Later the talks were published as the book *Mere Christianity*. Since its publication thousands of thoughtful people have found their way to a faith in Christ that makes sense. Included among these is Dr. Francis Collins, the scientist who broke the Genome, and also Charles Colson, President Nixon's chief of staff, and later founder of Prison Fellowship. *Mere Christianity* is for the thinking person. But the book appeals to the heart as well. In fact, it appeals to the whole person. It is not a surprise that this should be so.

In his literary criticism of his friend and fellow Inkling, Charles Williams' Arthurian Poems, *The Arthurian Torso*, C. S. Lewis said, "The first problem in life is how do you fit the stone [the Reason] and the shell [the Romantic longings of the heart]?" Lewis himself came to believe that Christianity did this best. In fact, after his long spell as an atheist, Lewis's first Christian book was titled, *The Pilgrim's Regress: An Allegorical Apology for Christianity, Reason and Romanticism*. He wrote to show that Christianity was a holistic faith that reconciled head and heart. This is because faith in Christ is a reconciling faith. It reconciles those estranged from God into a robust relationship with God. It gives the resources to make possible reconciliation of broken relationships with others. In fact, it provides the means to repair the ruins within one's own life. It sets the believer on the course of reconciling the soul and body as well as the head and the heart.

Lewis is known for his ability to open wardrobe doors into magical worlds where the themes of reconciliation are made accessible through children's stories like the Narnian Chronicles; written for children but very readable for adults. So too, one is grateful when someone comes along and opens a wardrobe door into an enriched understanding of Lewis's books.

This is what one encounters in Dr. Steven Urban's *Mere Christianity Study Guide: A Bible Study on the C. S. Lewis Book Mere Christianity.* With all of the diagnostic skill of a physician, Urban offers fresh insight on this Christian Classic making Lewis's thought all the more accessible for those who long to better understand Lewis and his ideas. Urban makes the book come alive with valuable applications for spiritual growth and maturity. In fact the book could be titled: C. S. Lewis's Spiritual Formation for Mere Christians. Urban is right to suggest that Lewis's book is not merely a work in Christian Apologetics and defense of the faith. Its themes are far richer than that. Lewis is concerned not only that the faith is defensible but it is also transformational. This fact is certainly developed by Dr. Urban.

Urban developed this study of *Mere Christianity* while teaching an adult Sunday school class. Over some time he developed the curriculum. Now, his treatment of *Mere Christianity* provides a valuable resource for the Church at large. All over the world Christians have studied *Mere Christianity* in Sunday schools and small groups around the globe. But never has such an in-depth study of the book been developed and made transferable for others to use while teaching from this classic text.

Urban has served well all who want such an aid to enhance their own teaching. I have been studying C. S. Lewis for 44 years. I have taught Lewis courses and lectured about Lewis for 34 years at 58 university campuses in 11 different countries around the world. Urban's study of Mere Christianity is the best I've seen.

It pleases me to see he is making his own study of Lewis available to others. You see, I've known Steve for over 35 years. My own grasp of Lewis was deeply influenced by things I learned from Steve while I was still in graduate school. It is high time others can have the privilege of gaining from his many years study of Lewis. I recommend the book for all who take their faith seriously and want to grow to be all they can be in Christ.

Jerry Root, PhD
Editor of *The Quotable C.S. Lewis*
Consulting Editor of *The C.S. Lewis Study Bible*

MERE CHRISTIANITY STUDY GUIDE
CHAPTER 1 SAMPLE

1. What is it that we can learn from people disagreeing or quarreling?

2. What are some of the different names Lewis says this can or has been called?

3. How is the Law of Human Nature different from other laws of nature?

4. Why in the past have people called this Rule about Right and Wrong the Law of Nature?

5. On what basis have some denied that the Law of (Human) Nature is known to all men?

6. How does Lewis respond to this denial?

7. Agreeing that Right and Wrong are *real or objective* and not merely a matter of taste, preference or opinion, what is the next point Lewis makes about our human Law of Nature?

8. Put Lewis's final summary into your own words:

THE SCREWTAPE LETTERS STUDY GUIDE
A Bible Study on the C.S. Lewis Book *The Screwtape Letters*
By Alan Vermilye

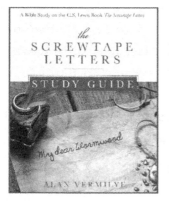

The Screwtape Letters Study Guide takes participants through a study of C.S. Lewis's classic, *The Screwtape Letters*.

This Bible study digs deep into each letter from Screwtape, an undersecretary in the lowerarchy of Hell, to his incompetent nephew Wormwood a junior devil. Perfect for small group sessions this interactive workbook includes daily, individual study with a complete answer guide available online.

Designed as a 12-week study, multiple week format options are also included.

What others are saying:

This book and study creates a positive reinforcement on fighting that Spiritual battle in life. Great read, great study guide! – Lester

This study guide was a wonderful way for our group to work through the Screwtape Letters! - Becky

Use this Study Guide for a Fresh "Seeing" of the Screwtape Letters! – William

This is an essential companion if you are reading The Screwtape Letters as a small group. – J.T.

THE SCREWTAPE LETTERS STUDY GUIDE
INTRODUCTION

For some time I wanted to read *The Screwtape Letters*. I would start, and then, for whatever reason, stop. Let's face it: some of Lewis' writings can be an intellectual exercise that require dedication to seeing them through. I would say this is especially true for me. However, having read his *Mere Christianity* several times and completing the *Mere Christianity Study Guide* by Steve Urban twice, I felt I was finally up to the challenge.

I committed myself to both reading the book and creating a Bible study guide for it. Recognizing the daunting task before me, I decided to lead the study at my own church while writing it. I knew this would help develop the study and provide the accountability I would desperately need to see it through.

The Screwtape Letters is not a very long book. There are 31 letters that are only five pages each and at the most six paragraphs. I began with research and found some insightful posts, commentaries, and a few discussion questions to help prime the pump. I also kept Google handy since Lewis was a very articulate man with a vast vocabulary.

Creating a Bible study around the content seemed to flow effortlessly. Obviously Lewis already provided excellent content; I simply had to draw parallels with various Scripture passages to help us relate to the main theme of each letter.

Facilitating group discussion at my church was probably the most valuable part of the experience. Not only did it help better refine the study, but I also learned from each class member as they shared their interpretation of what they read. I'm eternally grateful for their participation and input on the study.

THE SCREWTAPE LETTERS STUDY GUIDE
CHAPTER 1 SAMPLE

Summary

In this letter, we learn that Wormwood has been making sure that his patient spends plenty of time with his materialistic friends. Wormwood believes that by using reason and argument he can keep the man from belief in God. Screwtape does not disagree that it is good to influence the man's thoughts, but he reminds Wormwood that his main job is to keep the patient from thinking too deeply about any spiritual matter. Instead he should use ordinary everyday distraction to mislead the man.

Discussion Questions

1. In what way does Screwtape say that Wormwood is being naive?

2. What is Screwtape's explanation of why Wormwood should avoid reliance on "argument"?

3. What is the connection between "thinking and doing", and how does this impact our daily lives?

4. Screwtape claims that people "having a dozen incompatible philosophies dancing together inside their head". What specifically does he credit for this? What do you think the other "weapons" are today? How can they be used to destroy argument?

5. If, according to Screwtape, people are not persuaded by what is true or false, what does he say people are concerned with? Why do people believe what they believe?

6. Read Hebrews 2:14-18. What is the "abominable advantage" God has over Satan? How should this encourage us in our Christian walk?

7. The story of the atheist in the British museum provides a dark and somewhat disturbing insight into rather pleasant distractions that can draw us away from spiritual matters. In this particular instance, the atheist's appetite was enough to pull him away from his train of thought in which God was working. How can Satan use common distractions to create detours in the course of our daily lives?

8. Why would Screwtape advise Wormwood to "Keep pressing home on him the *ordinariness* of things."? What "comfort zones" in our Christian walk do we need to be cautious of?

9. Read Luke 10:39-42. What ordinary everyday distractions was Martha concerned with? Who did it make her resent? What did she miss out on?

THE GREAT DIVORCE STUDY GUIDE

A Bible Study on the C.S. Lewis Book *The Great Divorce*

By Alan Vermilye

The Great Divorce Study Guide is an 8-week Bible study on the C.S. Lewis classic, The Great Divorce. Perfect for small groups or individual study, each weekly study session applies a biblical framework to the concepts found in each chapter of the book. Although intriguing and entertaining, much of Lewis's writings can be difficult to grasp.

The Great Divorce Study Guide will guide you through each one of Lewis' masterful metaphors to a better understanding of the key concepts of the book, the supporting Bible passages, and the relevance to our world today. Each study question is ideal for group discussion and answers to each question are available online.

What others are saying:

To my knowledge, there have not been many study guides for either of these so to see this new one on "The Great Divorce" (both electronic and print) is a welcome sight! – Richard

I recommend the Great Divorce Study Guide to anyone or any group wishing to delve more deeply into the question, why would anyone choose hell over heaven! - Ruth

The questions were thought-provoking, and I very much liked how everything was evaluated by scripture. Would definitely recommend! – Justin

THE GREAT DIVORCE STUDY GUIDE
INTRODUCTION

What is the most desirable place you can think of to take a vacation? Perhaps it is a place that you have been before or someplace you dream of going. How would you respond if, once you arrived, you were invited to stay on this vacation forever? However, in order to stay, you must leave your old life behind. You cannot go back and say goodbye or set your affairs in order. You either must commit at that moment or return to your previous life.

How hard would it be for you to leave behind the life you are now living? It might be an easy decision for some and much more difficult for others.

In *The Great Divorce* by C.S. Lewis, damned spirits are given a vacation or a "holiday" away from Hell to visit Heaven, where they are invited to stay forever. There, they are persuaded by people they formally knew, relatives and friends, to come with them up the mountain to enjoy the bliss of Heaven. But they can only do so by leaving behind what is keeping them in Hell and accepting the love of God.

The answer seems obvious, right? Yet what we'll find is that it's not the choice to sin that binds people to Hell but rather the choice not to repent. We must let go, step out into the light, and embrace the better life that God has planned for us. That's the most confining part about sin—to admit you're in the wrong.

Lewis tells us not to take this story literally, nor does he suppose that eternity really is the way he presents it in the book. The fact is, Hell is final. Scripture records no opportunities offered after death to enter Heaven. On the title page of your book by Lewis, there is a telling quote from George MacDonald: "No, there is no escape. There is no heaven with a little of hell in it—no plan to retain this or that of the devil in our hearts or our pockets. Out Satan must go, every hair and feather."

In this story, Lewis quite vividly illustrates for us that we are all soul searching and our efforts either move us toward or away from God. It's a progression away from our own idea of what we think is best for us toward the humility required to embrace God's best for our lives. It can be painful to leave our old life behind, but with each step, it gets a little easier, and any pain will be nothing compared to the joy we will experience in Heaven.

I thoroughly enjoyed putting together this Bible study. As with all my studies, I write them for the small groups that I facilitate at my own church. Not only does it help better refine the study but I also learn from each class member as they share their interpretation of what they read. I'm eternally grateful for their participation and input on the study.

THE GREAT DIVORCE STUDY GUIDE
CHAPTER 1 SAMPLE

As the story begins, Lewis, also our narrator, finds himself waiting in a long line for a magical bus ride in a dismally uncomforting grey town. His companions in line are argumentative, combative, and generally disagreeable and of differing economic and educational backgrounds. As the story progresses we learn that these characters are damned souls on vacation, and that the grey town is Purgatory for some and the outskirts of Hell for others.

Discussion Questions

1. Describe in detail the mood, atmosphere, images, and depictions of the grey town. Do you find Lewis's depiction of Hell or Purgatory "accurate"?

2. Although the grey town is revealed within the contexts of the story to be the outer limits of Hell, or Purgatory for those who will eventually reach Heaven, the reader is to consider this an imaginative representation of Hell rather than an accurate, biblical representation of the real Hell. Using the following Bible passages, describe the nature of Hell. In your own words, how would you describe Hell to a friend?

   a) Revelation 14:10–11
   b) 2 Thessalonians 1:9
   c) Revelation 21:8
   d) Matthew 25:41

e) Mark 9:44–49

f) Revelation 20:10

g) Matthew 13:41–42

h) Matthew 3:12

i) Daniel 12:2

j) Luke 16:23–24

3. The souls that Lewis encounters while waiting for and getting on the bus seem to represent various forms of sin in what used to be called the capital sins or what is commonly referred to as the seven deadly sins. Associate the different personalities he encounters in line and on the bus with the appropriate sin below.

a) Envy – the desire to have an item, an experience, or feeling that someone else possesses

b) Gluttony – an excessive, ongoing consumption of food or drink

c) Greed – an excessive pursuit of material possessions

d) Lust – an uncontrollable passion or longing, especially for sexual desires

e) Vanity or Pride – excessive view of one's self without regard to others

f) Sloth – excessive laziness or the failure to act and utilize one's talents

g) Wrath or Anger – uncontrollable feelings of anger and hate toward another person

4. As people continue to leave the bus line, what principle is Lewis trying to establish regarding a town in which any real life is absent yet

there is little desire to move beyond it?

5. The souls complain about the bus driver, saying, "Why can't he behave naturally?" Read 1 Corinthians 2:14. Why do unbelievers have difficulty relating to or understanding a believer's joy?

6. The tousle-haired poet cannot imagine why the other souls would insist on coming on the bus and concludes that they would be much more comfortable at home. What parallel is there to our comfort and how we deal with sin? Read 1 John 1:8 and Romans 12:9. How do we break free of that sin comfort zone?

7. What do you think of Lewis's idea that there will be fish and chips and movies and advertising in Hell?

THE PROBLEM OF PAIN STUDY GUIDE

A Bible Study on the C.S. Lewis Book *The Problem of Pain*
By Alan Vermilye

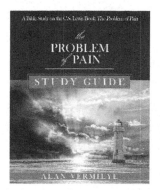

Why must humanity suffer? Why doesn't God alleviate our pain, even some?

In his book *The Problem of Pain*, C.S. Lewis's philosophical approach to why we experience pain can be confusing at times. The Problem of Pain Study Guide breaks down each chapter into easy-to-understand questions and commentary to help you find meaning and hope amid the pain.

The Problem of Pain Study Guide expands upon Lewis' elegant and thoughtful work where he seeks to understand how a loving, good, and powerful God can possibly coexist with the pain and suffering that is so pervasive in the world and in our lives. As Christ-followers we might expect the world to be just, fair, and less painful, but it is not. This is the problem of pain.

What others are saying:

Many thanks for lending me a helping hand with one of the greatest thinkers of all time! – Adrienne

The questions posed range from very straightforward (to help the reader grasp main concepts) to more probing (to facilitate personal application), while perhaps the greatest benefit they supply is their tie-in of coordinating scriptures which may not always be apparent to the reader. – Sphinn

The questions are thought-provoking and biblically based! – Jen

THE PROBLEM OF PAIN STUDY GUIDE
INTRODUCTION

The world suffers in pain. We take every precaution to escape it, but it's unavoidable. The fact is, we will experience some degree of pain and suffering in our lives. I was 19 when my mother lost her battle with cancer. Any faith I possessed at that time was suddenly rocked at the thought of losing her. In fact, I was angry and had a lot of questions. Many of those questions I expressed to her in the last few weeks of her life. I struggled with reconciling how a wonderful Christian woman could be taken in the prime of her life, especially while others, whom I perceived as evil, flourished. What's the point? What benefit does it serve?

You, too, have experienced pain—the death of loved ones, the betrayal of those closest to you, the loss of a job, a child in rebellion, the diagnoses that you were not expecting, and the list goes on.

Most often our pain results in a one-word question: Why? The answer is that we live in a fallen and evil world. Although this may be the root cause, it does little to comfort the one who is suffering.

I often wonder if the problem of pain would be easier to manage if I were not a Christian. If there's no higher power who has the ability to resolve my pain, then my only refuge is to exhaust every possible worldly option until I succeed or give up in defeat. But then I remember that in defeat, there's no more hope.

As a believer, I have hope because I know God is all-powerful and will resolve my pain in His time. Unfortunately, our pain also brings a certain amount of impatience, which leaves us wondering: Where is God in all of this? Does He hear my cries for help? Does He even care? Why is He allowing such pain and misery in my life?

In *The Problem of Pain*, C.S. Lewis sums up the problem of pain like this: "If God is good and all-powerful, why does he allow his creatures to suffer pain?" As Christians seeking to sincerely follow God, this sounds like a fair question.

Lewis does not claim to offer a complete solution to the problem of pain but rather takes a philosophical approach. He makes it very clear in the preface that his main purpose for writing the book is "to solve the intellectual problem raised by suffering" and not "to teach fortitude and patience while suffering." So if you're trying to understand the grieving process, this is not the book or study for you. Later Lewis would take a more personal approach in a reflection on his own experiences of grief and anguish at the death of his wife in *A Grief Observed*.

What Lewis does offer is a very detailed and thought out explanation of God's ability to use pain for our good while never dismissing the fact that pain hurts. Pain is a reliable friend that keeps us humble and dependent on God, and when that friend departs, we often find ourselves returning to a life of self-sufficiency and sin. Ultimately, Lewis challenges us to understand pain in the context of a God who provides meaning and hope in the person and work of Jesus Christ amid the pain. In His supreme act of self-surrender and love, He personally and profoundly experienced unjust pain and suffering to redeem our pain and suffering.

As His followers, we, too, are called to lives of submission and to walk as Jesus did. That walk will often include pain, although pain with a redemptive purpose. Perhaps as you have matured in your walk with Christ, you've been able to look back on your life and see how some of the worst experiences that you've had to endure have actually helped shape you into the person you are today.

THE PROBLEM OF PAIN STUDY GUIDE
CHAPTER 1 SAMPLE

Lewis starts this introductory chapter on a personal note: "Not many years ago when I was an atheist..." As an atheist, Lewis's objection to God was based on his observed futility of the universe, which included the mass proliferation of pain, suffering, and death of the human race.

He soon finds one problem in his observation: If the universe is as bad as he observes it to be, how could man have ever conceived of an all-loving God in the first place? No human being, destined to undergo pain and suffering and to be erased from all eternity, would ever think to connect it to an all-loving and caring God. Such a conception doesn't simply emerge out of the minds of men.

In the preface, Lewis's stated goal for the book is to "solve the intellectual problem raised by suffering." However, in order to do so, he must first examine the origin of religion and how it creates the problem of pain to begin with.

Discussion Questions

1. As a former atheist, how would Lewis have responded to anyone asking him why he did not believe in God? What had Lewis concluded about who or what created the universe? Given your own life experiences, have there been times when you struggled with the same question? Explain.

2. At the beginning of this chapter, Lewis uses a short quotation from Pascal, who criticizes the attempts of others to prove the existence of God from the works of nature. Pascal goes as far as to say that no "canonical writers" ever used nature to make a case for the existence of God. This, however, is incorrect. Read Psalm 29:3–6, Romans 1:20, Acts 14:15–17, and Job 12:7–9. According to Scripture, what does nature reveal, if anything, about God?

3. Regarding the universe, what was the one question that Lewis never dreamed of raising as an atheist?

4. Some might say that religion was developed in the fearful minds of our ignorant ancestors, who created the idea of a wise and good God. What does Lewis say is wrong with this assumption?

5. Lewis proposes that religion from its very beginning has included three elements (with Christianity proposing one more). The first element is the Numinous. Describe the Numinous. Why is the feeling of awe and dread of the supernatural (the Numinous) innate in all humans?

6. Using current and historical literature, Lewis states that we do not know how far back in human history the feeling of the supernatural goes. It somehow came into existence, is widespread, and "does not disappear from the mind with the growth of knowledge and civilization." How does our world today attempt to explain the

supernatural? What sources seek to influence our understanding of the supernatural?

7. Describe the second element found in all religions, the "moral experience." What is the one commonality found in all moralities throughout time?

8. Describe the third element found in all religions. Why is it not obvious why man would link the first two elements found in all religions?

9. Describe the historical incarnation, or the fourth element that is unique to Christianity.

10. Read John 10:30, John 8:58, Luke 22:70, Matthew 28:18, John 5:17–22, John 14:6, John 11:25, and Mark 14:61–62. Who does Jesus say that He is? What are the only two possible views of Jesus Christ?

11. How might becoming a Christian change your perception of God from awe and dread to hope?

12. How does not believing in Jesus Christ (the historical incarnation) impact your opinion of God?